Discovering Dinosaurs

GIANT MEAT-EATING DINOSAURS

Consulting Editor: Carl Mehling

Skyview Books

an imprint of
WINDMILL BOOKS
New York

Published in 2010 by Windmill Books, LLC
303 Park Avenue South, Suite # 1280, New York, NY 10010-3657

CREDITS:
Consulting Editor: Carl Mehling
Designer: Graham Beehag

Publisher Cataloging in Publication

Giant meat-eating dinosaurs / consulting editor, Carl Mehling.
    p. cm. – (Discovering dinosaurs)
Summary: With the help of fossil evidence this book provides physical descriptions of seventeen meat-eating dinosaurs.—Contents: Megalosaurus—Eustreptospondylus—Allosaurus—Yangchuanosaurus—Afrovenator—Acrocanthosaurus—Baryonyx—Utah Raptor—Giganotosaurus—Suchomimus—Carcharodontosaurus—Abelisaurus—Albertosaurus—Tyrannosaurus rex—Carnotaurus—Tarbosaurus—Majungatholus.
ISBN 978-1-60754-777-8. – ISBN 978-1-60754-785-3 (pbk.)
ISBN 978-1-60754-859-1 (6-pack)
1. Dinosaurs—Juvenile literature   2. Carnivora, Fossil—Juvenile literature
[1. Dinosaurs   2. Predatory animals]   I. Mehling, Carl   II. Series
567.9/12—dc22

Printed in the United States

CPSIA Compliance Information: Batch #BW10W: For further information contact Windmill Books, New York, New York at 1-866-478-0556.

CONTENTS

Introduction

Imagining what our world was like in the distant past is a lot like being a detective. There were no cameras around, and there were no humans writing history books. In many cases, fossils are all that remain of animals who have been extinct for millions of years.

Fossils are the starting point that scientists use to make educated guesses about what life was like in prehistoric times. And while fossils are important, even the best fossil can't tell the whole story. If snakes were extinct, and all we had left were their bones, would anyone guess that they could snatch bats from the air in pitch-black caves? Probably not, but there is a Cuban species of snake that can do just that. Looking at a human skeleton wouldn't tell you how many friends that person had, or what their favorite color was. Likewise, fossils can give us an idea of how an animal moved and what kind of food it ate, but they can't tell us everything about an animal's behavior or what life was like for them.

Our knowledge of prehistoric life is constantly changing to fit the new evidence we have. While we may never know everything, the important thing is that we continue to learn and discover. Learning about the history of life on Earth, and trying to piece together the puzzle of the dinosaurs, can help us understand more about our past and future.

Megalosaurus

ORDER • Saurischia • **FAMILY** • Megalosauridae • **GENUS & SPECIES** • *Megalosaurus bucklandii*

VITAL STATISTICS

FOSSIL LOCATION	England, Wales, France, Portugal
DIET	Carnivorous
PRONUNCIATION	MEG-ah-lo-SAWR-us
WEIGHT	1.3-2 tons (1.2-1.8 tonnes)
LENGTH	23-30 ft (7-9 m)
HEIGHT	10 ft (3 m)
MEANING OF NAME	"Great lizard" because of its large size

FOSSIL EVIDENCE

In 1676, part of a bone was discovered in an Oxfordshire quarry. It was first thought to be the thigh bone of a giant. More fossils were discovered in the early 1800s, but it was not until 1824 that scientists understood that the bones belonged to an enormous lizard-like creature. It was given the scientific name *Megalosaurus*, which means "great lizard." In 1842, the word "dinosaur" was created. Before scientists knew enough about dinosaurs to tell the difference between them, many dinosaur fossils were referred to as *Megalosaurus*.

DINOSAUR

MID JURASSIC

The first dinosaur to be described, *Megalosaurus* was also the first dinosaur to be given a scientific name. This happened before the word "dinosaur" had even been created.

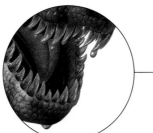

JAWS
Powerful jaws lined with curved, knife-like teeth could tear huge chunks of flesh from even the largest sauropods.

WHERE IN THE WORLD?

Megalosaurus fossils were first found in the limestone quarries and stonesfield slate of Oxfordshire in England.

LEGS
Megalosaurus walked upright on two muscular legs. A swift runner, this aggressive theropod possibly relied on surprise while hunting, rushing at its prey.

HOW BIG IS IT?

TIMELINE (millions of years ago)

40	505	438	408	360	280	248	208	146	65	1.8 to today

Eustreptospondylus

VITAL STATISTICS

FOSSIL LOCATION	England
DIET	Carnivorous
PRONUNCIATION	You-STREP-to-SPON-die-lus
WEIGHT	440-550 lb (200-250 kg)
LENGTH	23-30 ft (7-9 m)
HEIGHT	10-12 ft (3-3.7 m)
MEANING OF NAME	"True turned vertebrae" named for a form originally identified as a species of *Streptospondylus* which means "reversed vertebra" for the shape of its vertebrae

Eustreptospondylus was a typical theropod— a meat-eating monster that walked on two legs and could kill its victims with bloody efficiency. One interesting question is why its remains were found in sediment laid down on an ocean bottom—160 million years ago, southern England was made up of small islands in shallow seas. Was the carcass swept into the water, or did *Eustreptospondylus* sometimes plunge into the waves? It may have scavenged for dead bodies along beaches and estuaries, perhaps even wading in to grab fish and turtles. Or perhaps it learned to paddle with its back legs and swam between the islands.

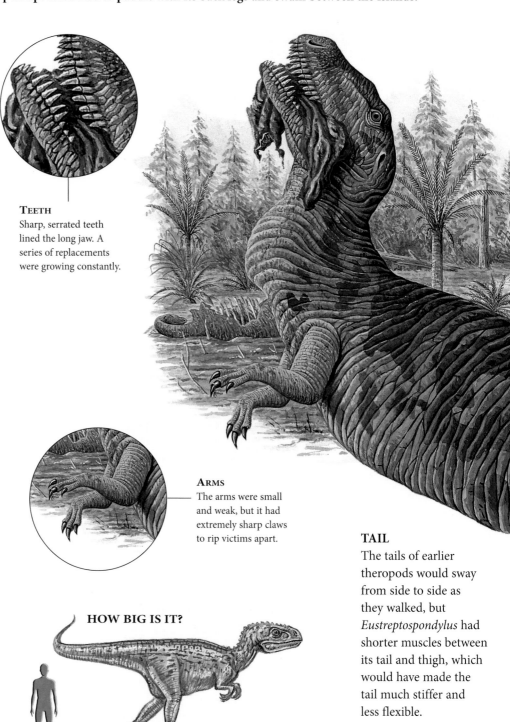

TEETH
Sharp, serrated teeth lined the long jaw. A series of replacements were growing constantly.

ARMS
The arms were small and weak, but it had extremely sharp claws to rip victims apart.

FOSSIL EVIDENCE

This is the best preserved theropod in Europe. It was first named as a *Megalosaurus* in 1841, but the mistake was corrected in 1964. The incomplete fossil is 16 ft (5 m) long, but the vertebrae show signs of not being fully developed, so it is thought to be a juvenile and to have been likely to grow another 6-13 ft (2-4 m). It has the powerful hind limbs, straight posture and small forelimbs characteristic of theropods. The skeleton is on display in England's Oxford University Museum.

DINOSAUR

MID JURASSIC

HOW BIG IS IT?

TAIL
The tails of earlier theropods would sway from side to side as they walked, but *Eustreptospondylus* had shorter muscles between its tail and thigh, which would have made the tail much stiffer and less flexible.

• **ORDER** • Saurischia • **FAMILY** • Megalosauridae • **GENUS & SPECIES** • *Eustreptospondylus oxoniensis*

WHERE IN THE WORLD?

A specimen was found in a clay pit north of Oxford in the UK.

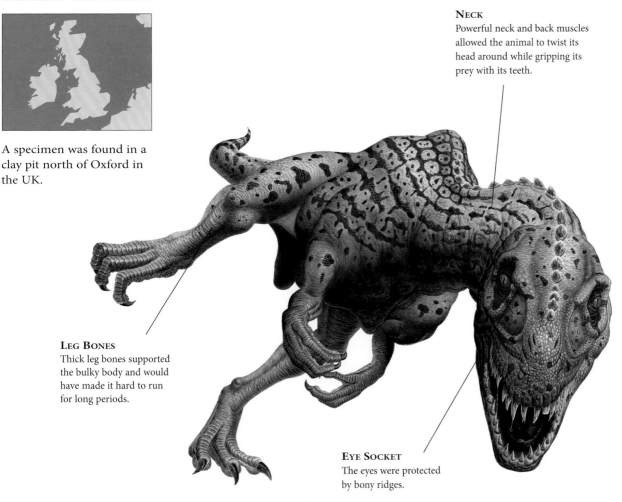

NECK
Powerful neck and back muscles allowed the animal to twist its head around while gripping its prey with its teeth.

LEG BONES
Thick leg bones supported the bulky body and would have made it hard to run for long periods.

EYE SOCKET
The eyes were protected by bony ridges.

HOLLOW HEAD

Eustreptospondylus might have bitten off large chunks of its prey's flesh, allowing it to feast while the victim bled to death. However, head weight could be a big problem for these giant monsters. In this creature that problem was solved by large hollow areas known as "fenestrae" in the skull. As a capable hunter, it is possible it lived alone apart from when it was time to mate.

ELINE (millions of years ago)

505	438	408	360	280	248	208	146	65	1.8 to today

Allosaurus

VITAL STATISTICS

FOSSIL LOCATION	United States and Europe
DIET	Carnivorous
PRONUNCIATION	Al-oh-SAWR-us
WEIGHT	2.5 tons (2.3 tonnes)
LENGTH	28 ft (8.5 m)
HEIGHT	13 ft (4 m)
MEANING OF NAME	"Strange lizard" because of its light vertebrae

FOSSIL EVIDENCE

Thousands of bones have been found, mainly in the US, together with footprints and possibly some eggs. Various species and ages of fossils reveal that Allosaurus grew into many different sizes. The measurements given are for a typical *Allosaurus fragilis*, the most common find, but the largest specimen is 32 ft (9.7 m) long. Larger sizes may belong to other species. *Allosaurus* had the typical large theropod features of a huge head, short S-shaped neck, shorter forelimbs and massive hind legs balanced by a long tail.

DINOSAUR

LATE JURASSIC

Allosaurus was a killing machine. Fast, powerful and able to attack anything it came across, it was the top predator for more than 10 million years. The many specimens found has allowed paleontologists to build a detailed picture of its body and lifestyle, but questions remain. How fast could it run? Although swift, it was top-heavy and risked serious injury if it fell onto its short front arms. Did it hunt in packs? Fossils have been found grouped together, but may have accumulated after death.

CURVED CLAWS

The front limbs had three sharp strongly curved claws capable of slicing through flesh, so at close range *Allosaurus* could possibly swipe at and kill its prey. The innermost claw was positioned like a thumb in that it was slightly apart from the others. The claws could be up to 6 in (15 cm) long. It also used its claws to seize flesh while it was eating.

HOW BIG IS IT?

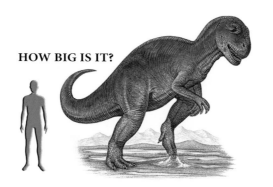

ORDER • Saurischia • **FAMILY** • Allosauridae • **GENUS & SPECIES** • Several possible species within the genus *Allosaurus*

BRINGING DOWN LARGER PREY

Allosaurus' fearsome teeth varied in size and shape. The biggest were 4 in (10 cm) and some were narrow and curved in the back, but all had saw-like edges. These would have been driven into prey, causing deep wounds and a lot of bleeding. This possibly allowed *Allosaurus* to attack animals larger than itself, taking a few savage bites and then waiting for its victim to collapse. It could open its hinged jaws very wide to swallow large chunks of flesh.

BALANCE
The tail was important for balance. Without its help, the top-heavy animal would fall and break its hollow forelimbs or ribs.

SPEED
The large muscular legs allowed it to sprint at prey, possibly popping out from tree cover close to waterholes where its victims drank.

WHERE IN THE WORLD?

Most specimens are from the Morrison Formation in the US, with others found in Portugal, and possibly Tanzania and Australia.

BRAIN
The brain was large in relation to its body weight, suggesting that *Allosaurus* was an intelligent dinosaur — far smarter than its victims, who were mostly herbivores.

MELINE (millions of years ago)

505	438	408	360	280	248	208	146	65	1.8 to today

Allosaurus

ORDER • Saurischia • **FAMILY** • Allosauridae • **GENUS & SPECIES** • Several possible species within the genus *Allosaurus*

THE MORRISON FORMATION

Although the fossils of the theropod dinosaur Allosaurus have been found in many places across the world, most have come from the Late Jurassic sedimentary rock of the Morrison Formation. The Formation, which centers in Wyoming and Colorado, covers an area of 600,000 square miles (1.5 million square kilometers). It was named after the town of Morrison in Colorado. In 1877, geologist Arthur Lakes sent a fossilized vertebra from the Formation to the paleontologist Othniel Charles Marsh, who identified it and named it Allosaurus. But the first large find of Allosaurus remains did not occur until 1883, when an almost complete skeleton was discovered by Marshall P. Felch, a rancher living in Fremont County, Colorado. Since then, more than 60 Allosaurus fossils of the common species *A. fragilis* have been discovered worldwide, most of them in the Morrison Formation. Several other dinosaurs have also been found, including *Ceratosaurus*, *Stegosaurus* and *Diplodocus*, while the megalosaur *Torvosaurus tanneri* was found in the area of the Formation comprising the Dry Mesa Quarry, Colorado, in 1971. *Torvosaurus*, one of North America's largest carnivores, was among the Quarry's first discoveries. It measured 36 ft (11 m) long and weighed in at 4400 lb (2000 kg).

Yangchuanosaurus

ORDER • Saurischia • **FAMILY** • Sinraptoridae • **GENUS & SPECIES** • *Yangchuanosaurus shangyoue*

VITAL STATISTICS

Fossil Location	China
Diet	Carnivorous
Pronunciation	YANG-choo-WAHN-oh-SAWR-us
Weight	5180 lb (2350 kg)
Length	20-33 ft (6-10 m)
Height	15 ft (4.6 m)
Meaning of name	"Yang-chu'an lizard" after the area in China where it was found

FOSSIL EVIDENCE

Yangchuanosaurus is one of the most complete fossil dinosaur skeletons ever found in China. Only an arm, a foot and a piece of its tail were missing. The position in which *Yangchuanosaurus'* fossil was found shows that after it died, the ligaments in its spine contracted and pulled the body into a "death pose." Its powerful jaws contained jagged teeth that could rip flesh and break bones. If one of its teeth broke off while attacking prey, another one later grew in its place.

DINOSAUR

LATE JURASSIC

In its time, *Yangchuanosaurus* was one of the largest predators living among stegosaurs and sauropods. It was classified as a carnosaur, a type of large, carnivorous theropod. *Yangchuanosaurus* probably hunted in packs.

SKULL
Yangchuanosaurus' large skull was not solid. It contained spaces, called fenestrae, which made the large head much lighter.

BACK
Some scientists think *Yangchuanosaurus* had a low crest on its spine, which would have given it a slightly hunchbacked appearance.

HOW BIG IS IT?

WHERE IN THE WORLD?

Yangchuanosaurus was uncovered during the construction of China's Shangyou Reservoir dam in Szechuan Province.

TIMELINE (millions of years ago)

540	505	438	408	360	280	248	208	146	65	1.8 to toda

Afrovenator

• ORDER • Saurischia **• FAMILY •** Megalosauridae **• GENUS & SPECIES •** *Afrovenator abakensis*

VITAL STATISTICS

FOSSIL LOCATION	Niger
DIET	Carnivorous
PRONUNCIATION	AF-roh-vee-NAY-tor
WEIGHT	1102 lb (500 kg)
LENGTH	26-30 ft (8-9 m)
HEIGHT	8 ft (2.5 m)
MEANING OF NAME	"African hunter"

Afrovenator was a relative of North America's *Allosaurus*. This link between African and North American dinosaurs tells us there could have been a land bridge between the two continents during the Early Cretaceous.

FOSSIL EVIDENCE

An almost whole *Afrovenator* fossil was discovered in Niger, making it the most complete skeleton of a Cretaceous carnivore from Africa found so far. *Afrovenator* was a carnivore that walked on two legs and had deadly claws. To balance its heavy front end, Afrovenator held its tail out stiffly behind it as it aggressively hunted prey. Its slender, graceful skeleton meant that *Afrovenator* was unusually agile for a theropod. This nimble dinosaur was also a vicious killer. Its remains were found with the fossil of a large sauropod that it may have attacked.

TEETH
A mouthful of sharp teeth, which each measuring 2 in (5 cm) long, made the bite of an *Afrovenator* absolutely deadly.

WHERE IN THE WORLD?

The Agadez Region of Niger, former home of *Afrovenator*, is now part of the Sahara Desert.

HOW BIG IS IT?

CLAWS
Afrovenator's claws were curved like sickles. The two largest claws on each hand were probably used to gouge and disembowel prey.

DINOSAUR

EARLY CRETACEOUS

MELINE (millions of years ago)

0	505	438	408	360	280	248	208	146	65	1.8 to today

Acrocanthosaurus

VITAL STATISTICS

FOSSIL LOCATION	United States
DIET	Carnivorous
PRONUNCIATION	AK-roh-CANthuh-SAWR-us
WEIGHT	5000 lb (2300 kg)
LENGTH	40 ft (12 m)
HEIGHT	16 ft (5 m)
MEANING OF NAME	"High spine lizard" due to the raised ridge on its spine

This was one of the largest of the theropods and is similar to the slightly smaller *Allosaurus* in its perfect qualities for killing prey. The main difference is that *Acrocanthosaurus* has a low fin of muscled spines that runs down its back.

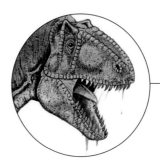

TEETH
The massive jaw was equipped with 68 sharp, curved serrated teeth perfectly suited to the task of tearing up flesh.

FOSSIL EVIDENCE

Some very large specimens, one with a skull nearly 4.3 ft (1.3 m) long, have been found. The long length of the femur bone suggests that *Acrocanthosaurus* probably could not run as quickly as some smaller dinosaurs. A fascinating dinosaur trackway in Texas is thought to be of this animal. The sets of fossilized prints seem to show a pack of *Acrocanthosaurus* stalking a herd of sauropods, but we don't know for sure. Large olfactory bulbs suggest that it could have hunted with its excellent sense of smell as well as its good eyesight.

RESTRICTED MOVEMENT

Close research into an entire fossilized arm shows us that the limb did not move very freely or with a wide range of movement. For example, *Acrocanthosaurus* could not reach its own neck. This suggests that when this dinosaur hunted, it led with its mouth, using its claws to grip and slash the already damaged victim wriggling in its jaws.

DINOSAUR

EARLY CRETACEOUS

• ORDER • Saurischia **• FAMILY •** Allosauridae or Carcharodontosauridae **• GENUS & SPECIES •** *Acrocanthosaurus atokensis*

SPIKES

Acrocanthosaurus had a set of long vertebral prongs running from the neck to the tail. Some over the back are 17 in (43 cm) high and they get shorter toward the tail. It seems that these were attached to powerful muscles that formed a thick fleshy ridge along its body rather like a fin. This could well have been brightly colored and used for signaling, fat storage or temperature control. It is far smaller than the skin sail of *Spinosaurus*, another large theropod.

WHERE IN THE WORLD?

Remains are mainly in Oklahoma and Texas, with some possibly in Maryland.

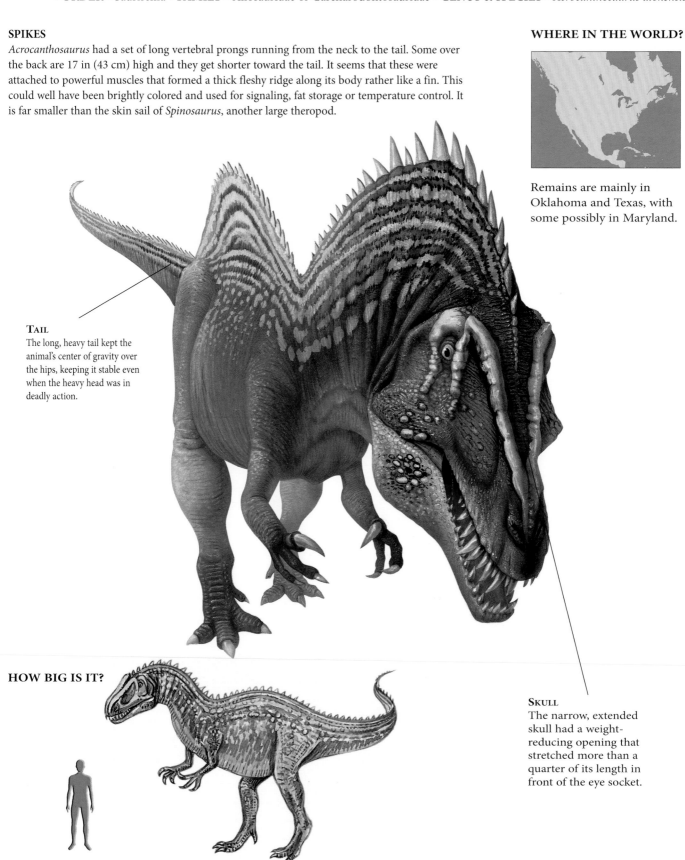

TAIL
The long, heavy tail kept the animal's center of gravity over the hips, keeping it stable even when the heavy head was in deadly action.

SKULL
The narrow, extended skull had a weight-reducing opening that stretched more than a quarter of its length in front of the eye socket.

HOW BIG IS IT?

TIMELINE (millions of years ago)

0	505	438	408	360	280	248	208	146	65	1.8 to today

Acrocanthosaurus

• ORDER • Saurischia **• FAMILY •** Allosauridae or Carcharodontosauridae **• GENUS & SPECIES •** *Acrocanthosaurus atokensis*

THE GRAND UNVEILING

The unveiling of the massive skeleton of *Acrocanthosaurus atokensis* on September 8, 1996, was an important event for the Black Hills Museum of Natural History in Hill City, South Dakota. It had taken years of hard work to take a find that had been buried in the bed of an ancient stream for some 120 million years into an exhibit worthy of its extraordinary importance. As Terry Wentz, one of the people who worked on the model, put it, "Even those of us involved in the preparation of this skeleton are awed by the sense of power we feel in (its) presence." This was not surprising, for *Acrocanthosaurus*, though slightly smaller, was a relative of the *Tyrannosaurus rex,* and was just as frightening. It took three years, between 1983 and 1986, for two amateur fossil collectors, Cephis Hall and Sidney Love, to excavate the huge skeleton of *Acrocanthosaurus* from a private site in McCurtain County in southeast Oklahoma. From there, the skeleton was taken to the Black Hills Institute in South Dakota, where the bones were carefully cleaned by experts and the skeleton restored. It was considered too valuable to risk by putting it on display, so a plaster copy was made.

Baryonyx

VITAL STATISTICS

FOSSIL LOCATION	Europe, Africa
DIET	Piscivorous
PRONUNCIATION	Bare-ee-ON-iks
WEIGHT	1750 lb (1700 kg)
LENGTH	28 ft (8.5 m)
HEIGHT	10 ft (3 m)
MEANING OF NAME	"Heavy claw" because of its massive claws

FOSSIL EVIDENCE

About 70 percent of the skeleton was recovered including, importantly, the skull that is so vital in building a detailed picture of the animal's appearance and lifestyle. Once *Baryonyx* was classified, many pieces of remains originally thought to be from the very similar *Suchosaurus* were assigned to it. The skeleton may not have been fully grown, so its adult measurements could have been larger than those given here, possibly as long as 37 ft (12 m) and as heavy as 7930 lb (3600 kg).

DINOSAUR

EARLY CRETACEOUS

In 1983 William Walker spotted a huge claw sticking out of a clay pit near Dorking in Surrey, England. As an amateur fossil hunter he knew the 1 ft (30 cm) specimen was something special. Eventually, an almost complete skeleton of a new species of dinosaur was found at the site, and it was named after its finder. *Baryonyx walkeri* is unusual because it is one of the few non-avian dinosaurs that we think ate fish, possibly sitting on a riverbank and swiping them out of the water with a massive claw, in a similar manner to the salmon-catching bears of today.

ARMS
The long, strong arms suggest that *Baryonyx* could walk on all fours, and if so, would make it the only theropod known to do so.

HOW BIG IS IT?

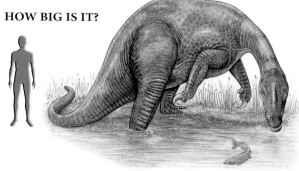

• **ORDER** • Saurischia • **FAMILY** • Spinosauridae • **GENUS & SPECIES** • *Baryonyx walkeri*

CROCODILE CHARACTERISTICS

The skull and long, flat jaw have features that are similar to a crocodile. The skull had twice as many teeth as many of its relatives did — 64 in the lower jaw, 32 larger ones in the upper jaw. The notch near the snout is a crocodilian feature probably designed to stop prey from escaping. There was a small crest on the top of the head.

WHERE IN THE WORLD?

Fossils have been discovered in England, Portugal and western Africa.

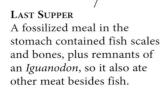

NECK
The neck was long, straight and less flexible than the S-shaped necks of most theropods.

LAST SUPPER
A fossilized meal in the stomach contained fish scales and bones, plus remnants of an *Iguanodon*, so it also ate other meat besides fish.

FORELIMB

Each forelimb ended with a curved claw, like a scimitar, 12 in (30 cm) long. This thumb-claw was possibly used to spear and scoop fish from the water, just like grizzly bears of North America. It may have sat at the edge of the water ready to leap with its powerful legs. This enormous blade could also have been useful for picking at the remains of dead animals because it is likely that *Baryonyx* also scavenged for food on the plains and deltas of what is now northern Europe.

MELINE (millions of years ago)

0	505	438	408	360	280	248	208	146	65	1.8 to today

Utahraptor

VITAL STATISTICS

Fossil Location	United States
Diet	Carnivorous
Pronunciation	YOU-ta-RAP-tor
Weight	150 lb (700 kg)
Length	21 ft (6.5 m)
Height	6.6 ft (2 m)
Meaning of name	"Utah thief" after the site where it was discovered

FOSSIL EVIDENCE

The well-preserved and almost complete skeleton was discovered at a quarry near Moab in 1991 and named in 1993. *Utahraptor* was a dromaeosaurid, a group of light, quick-moving and smart dinosaurs with large brains, good senses, and a killing claw on each foot. Fossil finds of several of these dromaeosaurids around giant plant-eaters suggest they were able to hunt in packs, disabling their victim with numerous stabs and cuts. They were bipedal and may have been at least partly covered with feathers.

DINOSAUR

EARLY CRETACEOUS

Meeting a *Utahraptor* was bad news for the herbivores of the Early Cretaceous Period. Possibly one of the smartest dinosaurs of its time, it was fast and agile and had a pair of formidable toe claws.

SKULL
The skull was 18 in (45 cm) long and it had large eyes as well as a large brain.

CONFIDENT PREDATOR
The second toe had a sickle-like claw that was 9-15 in (23-38 cm) long. Large joints held it upright while the animal moved, helping it stay sharp.

HOW BIG IS IT?

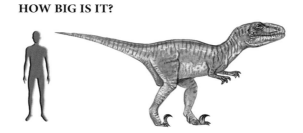

• ORDER • Saurischia **• FAMILY •** Dromaeosauridae **• GENUS & SPECIES •** *Utahraptor ostrommaysorum*

FINE BODY RODS

The long, thick tail was stiffened by fine bony rods so it would have been almost rigid. It probably worked like an acrobat's pole to help *Utahraptor* keep stable while running.

WHERE IN THE WORLD?

The remains were found at a quarry in Grand County, Utah. Some possible pieces have been found in South America.

CLAWS
Each hand held three broad, flat talon-like claws that could pierce flesh to provide a strong grip.

TEETH
The jagged teeth were 2 in (5 cm) long and set in a powerful jaw that could crush victims or cut through flesh. New teeth grew to replace any that broke.

TIMELINE (millions of years ago)

40	505	438	408	360	280	248	208	146	65	1.8 to today

Utahraptor

• **ORDER** • Saurischia • **FAMILY** • Dromaeosauridae • **GENUS & SPECIES** • *Utahraptor ostrommaysorum*

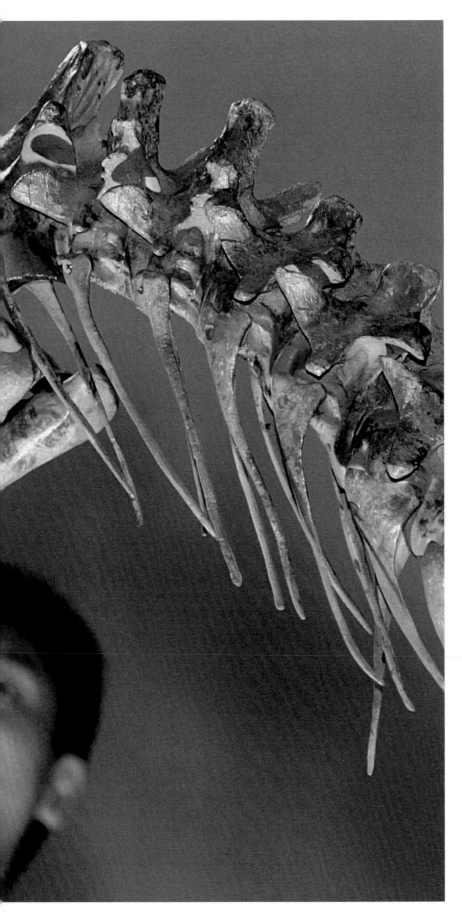

FOOTPRINTS TELL A STORY

Dinosaur remains are not only fossils. Dinosaur footprints, or "trackways" as they are also called, also have a great deal to tell. Footprints left behind by *Utahraptor ostrommaysorum* have been discovered in a coal mine in Utah, some of them alone and some with many prints, showing that many *Utahraptor* walked this way millions of years ago. In one trackway, footprints were discovered showing where 23 *Utahraptor* moved across what was in prehistoric times a peat bog, but now lies deep beneath a mountain. One of the footprints was left by a *Utahraptor* 10 ft (3 m) tall, 20 ft (6 m) long and weighing more than 1500 lb (680 kg). Another *Utahraptor* left an impression of its large heel in the ancient peat. Further on, though, the trail of heel prints became fainter until they stopped marking the peat altogether. From this, paleontologists think that the *Utahraptor* was running toward its prey, with its heel lifting away from the peat as it neared its victim. A further set of *Utahraptor* footprints showed that each of the 14 steps the dinosaur took was exactly 3.5 ft (109 cm) apart.

Giganotosaurus

• **ORDER** • Saurischia • **FAMILY** • Carcharodontosauridae • **GENUS & SPECIES** • *Giganotosaurus carolir*

VITAL STATISTICS

FOSSIL LOCATION	Argentina
DIET	Carnivorous
PRONUNCIATION	GI-gan-ot-oh-SAWR-us
WEIGHT	Up to 8.8 tons (9.7 tonnes)
LENGTH	46 ft (14 m)
HEIGHT	Unknown
MEANING OF NAME	"Giant lizard of the south"

Giganotosaurus is one of the largest carnivores ever to have roamed the land, bigger even than *Tyrannosaurus rex*. In a skull 6 ft (1.8 m) long, its brain was the size and shape of a banana.

WHERE IN THE WORLD?

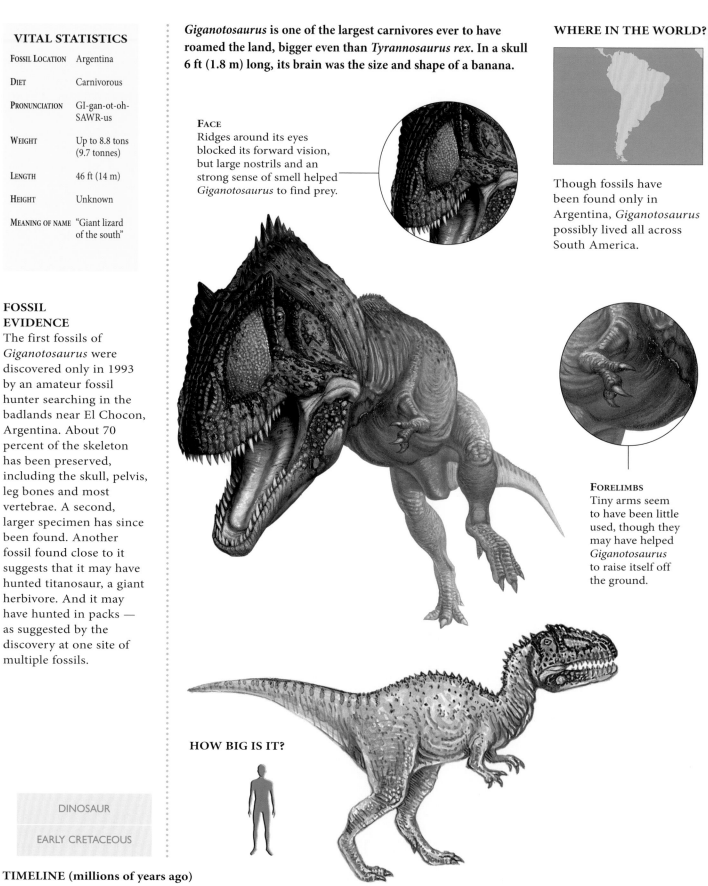

Though fossils have been found only in Argentina, *Giganotosaurus* possibly lived all across South America.

FACE
Ridges around its eyes blocked its forward vision, but large nostrils and an strong sense of smell helped *Giganotosaurus* to find prey.

FOSSIL EVIDENCE

The first fossils of *Giganotosaurus* were discovered only in 1993 by an amateur fossil hunter searching in the badlands near El Chocon, Argentina. About 70 percent of the skeleton has been preserved, including the skull, pelvis, leg bones and most vertebrae. A second, larger specimen has since been found. Another fossil found close to it suggests that it may have hunted titanosaur, a giant herbivore. And it may have hunted in packs — as suggested by the discovery at one site of multiple fossils.

FORELIMBS
Tiny arms seem to have been little used, though they may have helped *Giganotosaurus* to raise itself off the ground.

DINOSAUR

EARLY CRETACEOUS

HOW BIG IS IT?

TIMELINE (millions of years ago)

540	505	438	408	360	280	248	208	146	65	1.8 to today

Suchomimus

• ORDER • Saurischia **• FAMILY •** Spinosauridae **• GENUS & SPECIES •** *Suchomimus tenerensis*

VITAL STATISTICS

FOSSIL LOCATION	Africa
DIET	Carnivorous
PRONUNCIATION	Soo-koe-MY-mus
WEIGHT	6 tons (6 tonnes)
LENGTH	40 ft (12 m)
HEIGHT	13 ft (4 m)
MEANING OF NAME	"Crocodile mimic" because of its crocodile-like mouth

FOSSIL EVIDENCE

Although it had a mouth like a crocodile and nostrils on top of the snout, the rest of *Suchomimus* was more like *T. rex* — big and powerful with a long, strong tail. The forelimbs had a huge curved thumb. It was very similar to *Baryonyx*, apart from the tail spines on its backbone.

Suchomimus was a big, powerful predator that may have caught fish in the lush swamps of what is now the Sahara, wading in to trap them in its claws or jaws.

SPINES
Tail spines along the backbone may have supported a fleshy fin used for display and possibly to help it warm up and cool down.

WHERE IN THE WORLD?

Found in 1997 in the Sahara, near the Tenere Desert of Niger, in eastern Africa.

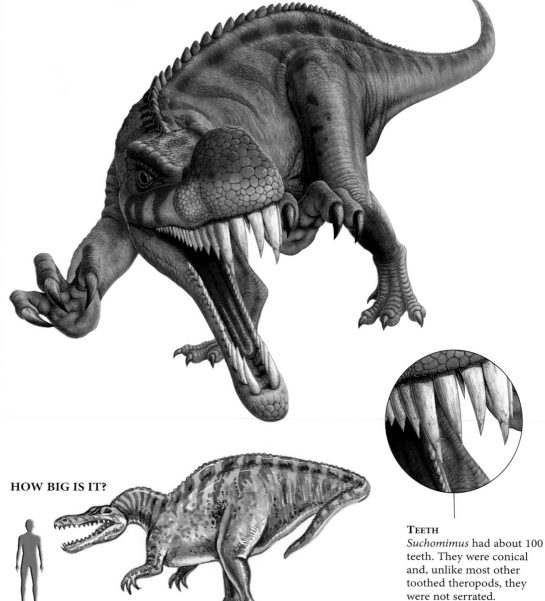

HOW BIG IS IT?

DINOSAUR

EARLY CRETACEOUS

TEETH
Suchomimus had about 100 teeth. They were conical and, unlike most other toothed theropods, they were not serrated.

MELINE (millions of years ago)

0	505	438	408	360	280	248	208	146	65	1.8 to today

Carcharodontosaurus

VITAL STATISTICS

Fossil Location	Africa
Diet	Carnivorous
Pronunciation	Car-car-owe-dont-owe-SORE-us
Weight	1315 lb (2900 kg)
Length	44 ft (13.5 m)
Height	12 ft (3.65 m)
Meaning of name	"*Carcharodon* tooth lizard" because its teeth look like those of *Carcharodon*, the great white shark, whose name, in turn, means "jagged toothed"

FOSSIL EVIDENCE

Carcharodontosaurus is among the most gigantic meat-eating dinosaurs ever discovered. Its jaws were huge and contained teeth that were up to 8 in (20 cm) long. *Carcharodontosaurus saharicus'* skull was 5.5 ft (1.75 m) long; the skull of *C. iguidensis* was longer, at 6.5 ft (1.95 m). The only small part of this predator were its short arms, but even they were dangerous weapons, carrying three-fingered, sharp-clawed hands. In addition, *Carcharodontosaurus* was possibly a fast runner, able to catch its prey with terrifying speed.

DINOSAUR

MID CRETACEOUS

Carcharodontosaurus arrived on the paleontological scene in 1927, when a skull and a few bones were found in the Sahara Desert of northern Africa. It was first named *Megalosaurus saharicus*, which meant "huge Sahara lizard" but was renamed by the German paleontologist Ernst Stromer in 1931. Like the ill-fated remains of *Spinosaurus*, the *Carcharodontosaurus* fossils were destroyed when the Munich museum housing them was bombed by the British during World War II. Fortunately, the famous American paleontologist Paul Sereno and his team made another, even larger find in North Africa in 1996.

SMALL BRAIN

Carcharodontosaurus might have had a huge skull, but its brain was very small — smaller than the brain of *Tyrannosaurus rex*, with which it is often compared. Paleontologists can study *Carcharodontosaurus'* brain with endocast, or endocranial cast, which is a cast made from the impression made by the brain on the inside of the braincase. Such a cast lets paleontologists study dinosaur brains without damaging the original skull.

HOW BIG IS IT?

• **ORDER** • Saurischia • **FAMILY** • Carcharodontosauridae • **GENUS & SPECIES** • *Carcharodontosaurus saharicus, C. iguidensis*

TEETH DISCOVERY

The destruction of the Munich museum in a bombing raid in 1944 left paleontologists with a puzzle that took more than half a century to solve, until paleontologist Paul Sereno matched the teeth from his 1996 Moroccan find with those described by Ernst Stromer in 1915. This proved that Stromer's finds and Sereno's discoveries belonged to the same predator.

Fossils have been found in Morocco and Niger.

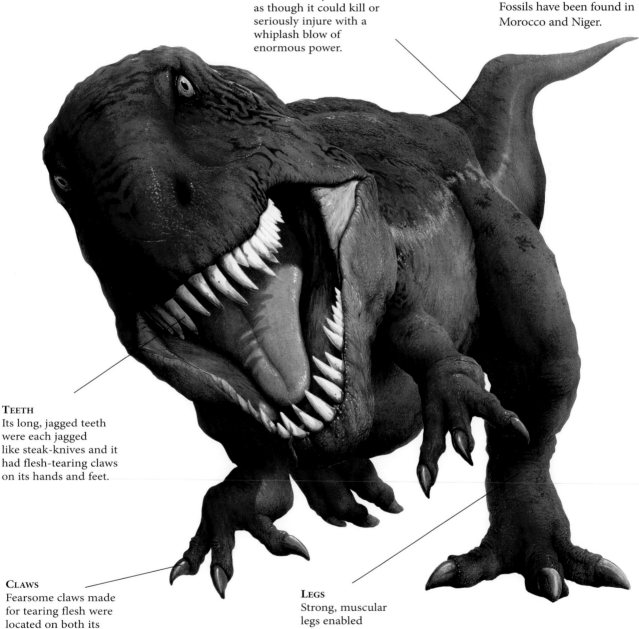

TAIL
A thick, heavy tail looked as though it could kill or seriously injure with a whiplash blow of enormous power.

TEETH
Its long, jagged teeth were each jagged like steak-knives and it had flesh-tearing claws on its hands and feet.

CLAWS
Fearsome claws made for tearing flesh were located on both its hands and feet.

LEGS
Strong, muscular legs enabled *Carcharodontosaurus* to move quickly.

MELINE (millions of years ago)

| 505 | 438 | 408 | 360 | 280 | 248 | 208 | 146 | 65 | 1.8 to today |

Carcharodontosaurus

• ORDER • Saurischia • **FAMILY •** Carcharodontosauridae • **GENUS & SPECIES •** *Carcharodontosaurus saharicus, C. iguidensis*

HUGE CARNIVORE

The most exciting event in paleontology is the discovery of an unknown species. This is what happened in 1997, when the remains of a huge meat-eating dinosaur, *Carcharodontosaurus*, were found in the Republic of Niger in northwest Africa. The announcement of the new species, named *Carcharodontosaurus iguidensis,* was not made until December 2007, but it gave paleontologists what may be one of the biggest carnivores that ever lived. *C. Iguidensis* was thought to measure around 44 ft (13.5 m) long, with a skull some 5.5 ft (1.75 m) in length and had a mouth packed with teeth the size of bananas. The find was made up of several pieces of skull including parts of the snout, the lower jaw and the braincase, and part of the great dinosaur's neck. *Carcharodontosaurus iguidensis* lived around 95 million years ago, when levels of the Earth's seas and oceans were the highest they have ever been. In addition, the climate was the warmest it had ever been. As a result, Niger and Morocco, where the previous *Carcharodontosaurus* finds had been made in 1996, were separated from each other, allowing the Niger dinosaurs to evolve in different ways from the Moroccan ones.

Abelisaurus

• **ORDER** • Saurischia • **FAMILY** • Abelisauridae • **GENUS & SPECIES** • *Abelisaurus comahuen*

VITAL STATISTICS

Fossil Location	Argentina
Diet	Carnivorous
Pronunciation	Ah-beli-i-SAWR-us
Weight	1.4 tons (1.4 tonnes)
Length	21–26 ft (6.5–7.9 m)
Height	6 ft (2 m) at the hips
Meaning of name	"Abel's lizard" after Roberto Abel, who discovered it

FOSSIL EVIDENCE

Only part of a skull was found in 1985. Models are based on the structures of other bipedal carnivores with a similarly large head, so it is assumed to have slender legs, short front limbs and a long tail, which balanced the weight of the skull. The major difference between *Abelisaurus* and the tyrannosaurids of the Northern Hemisphere is the large gap in front of the eyes. It was one of South America's fiercest predators, using its speed to pounce on the slower plant-eaters and tearing at their flesh with its many teeth.

DINOSAUR

LATE CRETACEOUS

This was an early theropod, a two-legged meat-eater, which is interesting because it shows such creatures probably evolved separately in the Southern and the Northern Hemisphere.

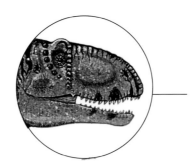

TEETH
The teeth are smaller than those of a *T. Rex* and quite heavy.

WHERE IN THE WORLD?

Found in the Anacleto Formation in the Rio Negro Province of Argentina.

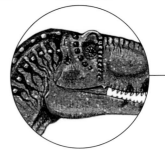

SKULL
The 33 in (85 cm) skull features large window-like openings (fenestrae) to reduce its weight.

HOW BIG IS IT?

TIMELINE (millions of years ago)

540	505	438	408	360	280	248	208	146	65	1.8 to today

Albertosaurus

• **ORDER** • Saurischia • **FAMILY** • Tyrannosauridae • **GENUS & SPECIES** • *Albertosaurus sarcophagus*

VITAL STATISTICS

FOSSIL LOCATION	North America
DIET	Carnivorous
PRONUNCIATION	Al-BER-toe-SAWR-us
WEIGHT	1.4–1.9 tons (1.3–1.7 tonnes)
LENGTH	30 ft (9 m)
HEIGHT	11 ft (3.4 m) at the hips
MEANING OF NAME	"Alberta lizard" after the Canadian province where many were found

This theropod was a close relative of *Tyrannosaurus rex*, which appeared a few million years later. It was half the size of its later distant cousin and a speedy runner, possibly capable of 25-30 mph (40-48 km/h).

JAW
The lower jaw had 14–16 saw-edged teeth and the upper jaw had 17–19. Each tooth had a another growing under it, ready to replace broken or worn-out ones.

WHERE IN THE WORLD?

Alberta in Canada, plus Montana and Wyoming.

FOSSIL EVIDENCE

The finding of several individuals aged from two to 28 years of age on the same site has led some paleontologists to suggest that *Albertosaurus* hunted in packs, possibly family groups, with the faster young dinosaurs herding prey toward the larger, slower elders. Its two-fingered arms were not very useful, and were too short to reach its mouth, so it would have led attacks with its gaping jaw. *Albertosaurus* also possibly had a good sense of smell, which would have allowed it to scavenge for dead meat, hunting by scent.

EYES
While its body structure was similar to *T. rex*, its eyes were positioned more toward the sides, making it harder for it to judge distances.

HOW BIG IS IT?

DINOSAUR

LATE CRETACEOUS

TIMELINE (millions of years ago)

0	505	438	408	360	280	248	208	146	65	1.8 to today

Tyrannosaurus rex

VITAL STATISTICS

FOSSIL LOCATION	North America
DIET	Carnivorous
PRONUNCIATION	Tee-RAN-oh-sawr-us rex
WEIGHT	7 tons (7000 kg)
LENGTH	43 ft (13 m)
HEIGHT	13 ft (4 m)
MEANING OF NAME	"Tyrant lizard" because of its huge size (rex means king)

FOSSIL EVIDENCE

One of the first discoveries of the fossils of *Tyrannosaurus rex* occurred in 1874, when some of its 13 in (33 cm) long teeth were found in Colorado. In 1890, bones from *Tyrannosaurus'* skull were found in Wyoming, followed in 1892 by pieces of its backbone (vertebra). Wyoming was also where the first partial skeleton of *Tyrannosaurus* was found in 1900.

DINOSAUR

LATE CRETACEOUS

The fearsome *Tyrannosaurus rex* is probably the most famous dinosaur of them all. Tyrannosaurus rex is usually considered to be the greatest meat-eater of all time, although it was not the largest dinosaur. (Some larger theropods include *Spinosaurus*, *Carcharodontosaurus*, and *Giganotosaurus*.) *Tyrannosaurus* was 43 ft (13 m) long.

NECK
Tyrannosaurus rex's short, thick neck had powerful muscles to support the dinosaur's oversized head.

ARMS
Paleontologists have not been able to agree on the function of *Tyrannosaurus'* tiny arms and two-fingered hands.

HOW BIG IS IT?

• **ORDER** • Saurischia • **FAMILY** • Tyrannosauridae • **GENUS & SPECIES** • *Tyrannosaurus rex*

WHERE IN THE WORLD?

Tyrannosaurus rex was found throughout western North America.

BALANCING ABILITY

Tyrannosaurus rex's ability to stand upright required a balancing act. The tail, which contained up to 40 vertebrae, was big and heavy and balanced its torso and enormous head, which could be up to 5 ft (1.5 m) long. However, many bones in *Tyrannosaurus'* body were hollow to make up for the dinosaur's enormous bulk. Its big, muscle-bound legs were some of the longest seen in any dinosaur compared to the size of its body. *Tyrannosaurus'* skull bones also had tiny air spaces, which made them lighter.

LEGS

It was once thought that *Tyrannosaurus* walked slowly on its large legs, but paleontologists now think that it may have been a fast runner.

COLOSSAL TEETH

Tyrannosaurus rex had bigger teeth than any other carnivorous dinosaur. The teeth in the upper jaw were larger than most of the teeth in the lower jaw, the largest measuring 13 in (33 cm) from root to sharp, pointed tip. Some of *T. rex's* other teeth were shaped like blades with chiseled tips. The teeth at the front of the upper jaw were closely packed together.

IELINE (millions of years ago)

| 505 | 438 | 408 | 360 | 280 | 248 | 208 | 146 | 65 | 1.8 to today |

Tyrannosaurus rex

• **ORDER** • Saurischia • **FAMILY** • Tyrannosauridae • **GENUS & SPECIES** • *Tyrannosaurus rex*

HOW LONG DID *TYRANNOSAURUS* LIVE?

For a species to survive, it must have many members. This may have been the case for *Tyrannosaurus rex*. Many, if not most, *Tyrannosaurus* survived their first few years. Some paleontologists have suggested that the mortality rate among juvenile *Tyrannosaurus* was low. They believe this because relatively few *Tyrannosaurus rex* juveniles have been found in fossilized form, which suggest that juveniles did not die in large numbers. But, it is important to remember that there could be many other reasons for their poor fossil record. At age 14, a young *Tyrannosaurus* began to grow quite dramatically, and though growth began to slow by about age 16, it could gain 13000 lb (6000 kg) by the time it was approximately 18 years old. By then, paleontologists think that *Tyrannosaurus rex* had reached maturity and was able to start reproducing. But it may have had only 6–10 years to do so; the average *Tyrannosaurus rex* only lived about 28 years.

Carnotaurus

VITAL STATISTICS

FOSSIL LOCATION	South America
DIET	Carnivorous
PRONUNCIATION	Car-no-TAWR-us
WEIGHT	620 lb (1730 kg)
LENGTH	25 ft (7.5 m)
HEIGHT	9 ft (2.7 m)
MEANING OF NAME	"Meat-eating bull" because of its flesh-eating habit and bull-like horns

FOSSIL EVIDENCE

A single almost complete skeleton of *Carnotaurus* was discovered and named in 1985. Scientists were able to describe the skin along *Carnotaurus'* entire right side, which, unlike some similar coelurosaurian theropods, seems to have had no feathers. Instead, the skin had rows of bumps that became larger the closer they were to the dinosaur's spine.

DINOSAUR

LATE CRETACEOUS

Carnotaurus lived in the Cretaceous Period about 90 million years ago. *Carnotaurus sastrei* is the only known species of this strange-looking dinosaur that we know of. Its head looked almost like a bulldog and the horns on top of its head looked like those of a bull. *Carnotaurus'* arms were unusually short and it had very small four-fingered hands. Unlike most other dinosaurs, *Carnotaurus'* eyes faced a little way forward, so it probably had a limited form of binocular vision. This meant that it could use both eyes to see some vision in depth.

HORNS
The bull-like horns were probably used during mating rituals or to head-butt rivals and drive them away.

TIMELINE (millions of years ago)

540	505	438	408	360	280	248	208	146		65	1.8 to toda

• **ORDER** • Saurischia • **FAMILY** • Abelisauridae • **GENUS & SPECIES** • *Carnotaurus sastrei*

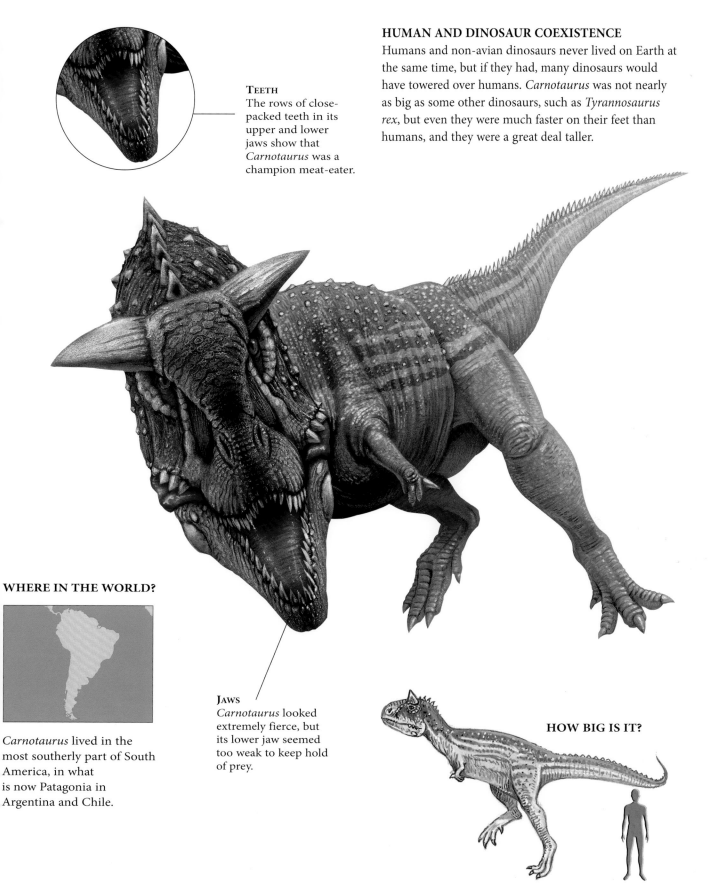

TEETH
The rows of close-packed teeth in its upper and lower jaws show that *Carnotaurus* was a champion meat-eater.

HUMAN AND DINOSAUR COEXISTENCE

Humans and non-avian dinosaurs never lived on Earth at the same time, but if they had, many dinosaurs would have towered over humans. *Carnotaurus* was not nearly as big as some other dinosaurs, such as *Tyrannosaurus rex*, but even they were much faster on their feet than humans, and they were a great deal taller.

WHERE IN THE WORLD?

Carnotaurus lived in the most southerly part of South America, in what is now Patagonia in Argentina and Chile.

JAWS
Carnotaurus looked extremely fierce, but its lower jaw seemed too weak to keep hold of prey.

HOW BIG IS IT?

Carnotaurus

• **ORDER** • Saurischia • **FAMILY** • Abelisauridae • **GENUS & SPECIES** • *Carnotaurus sastrei*

WEIRDEST DINOSAUR EVER?

South America has proved to be the home of some very unusual dinosaurs, and *Carnotaurus* is a prime example. Some think it could be called the "Weirdest Dinosaur Ever." *Carnotaurus* was an abelisaurid and belonged to a group of theropods with deep skulls and snouts and a mouthful of large, blade-shaped teeth. The abelisaurid, which gives its name to the group *Abelisaurus* (Greek for "Abel's lizard,") was named after its discoverer, Roberto Abel, one-time director of the Museo de Cipolletti, Argentina. Despite its deep skull, *Carnotaurus'* lower jaw was thin and weak, and the upper jaw was unusually short, giving Carnotaurus its distinctly snub-nosed profile. By contrast, *Carnotaurus'* neck was unusually long for a theropod, and it also had strange arms. Paleontologists are puzzled as to how the dinosaur could have used them, if it used them at all. Like so many dinosaurs, *Carnotaurus'* arms were tiny compared to its overall size. The upper arm seemed strong enough, but the two forearms were extremely short and the whole arrangement appeared very stunted, as did *Carnotaurus'* hands. One of its four fingers was little more than a backward-facing spike and the palms faced outward.

Tarbosaurus

VITAL STATISTICS

FOSSIL LOCATION	Mongolia, China
DIET	Carnivorous
PRONUNCIATION	Tar-boh-SAWR-us
WEIGHT	10800 lb (4900 kg)
LENGTH	33 ft (10 m)
HEIGHT	16 ft (5 m)
MEANING OF NAME	"Terrifying lizard"

FOSSIL EVIDENCE

In 1946, the Soviet Union and Mongolia teamed up to send an expedition into the Gobi Desert, where it found a large skull along with some back bones belonging to a member of the theropod group. Three more skulls were discovered there in 1948 and 1949. These finds were classed in 1965 as different stages of the same species, *Tarbosaurus bataar* ("Tarbosaurus the hero"). After that, expeditions from Poland, Japan and Canada, as well as from Mongolia itself began digging in Mongolia's Nemegt Formation. So far, more than 30 *Tarbosaurus* fossils have been found, together with 15 skulls.

DINOSAUR

LATE CRETACEOUS

Tarbosaurus, a smaller relative of the famous *Tyrannosaurus rex*, lived on the humid floodplains of Mongolia and China around 75 million years ago. Like its relatives, it was a strong predator, and may have taken on dinosaurs much larger than itself, such as the hadrosaurs. Like *Tyrannosaurus*, *Tarbosaurus* moved around on two legs, and it was a major predator. However, *Tarbosaurus'* arms and two-fingered hands were the smallest found in any dinosaur of the Tyrannosaurid family.

SMALL HANDS
Like all later tyrannosaurs, Tarbosaurus had short arms and only two clawed fingers on its hands. Although some scientists think the tyrannosaur arms were very strong, others believe they were vestigial and of not very important to the group.

HOW BIG IS IT?

CLAWS
Tarbosaurus had three sharp, curved 4.5 in (11.4 cm) long claws on each of its back feet and two on each of its fore feet.

• **ORDER** • Saurischia • **FAMILY** • Tyrannosauridae • **GENUS & SPECIES** • *Tarbosaurus bataar*

TEETH
Tarbosaurus had up to 64 sharp teeth in its jaws, the largest, in the upper jawbone, were 3 in (8.5 cm) long.

WHERE IN THE WORLD?

Tarbosaurus was found in the Nemegt Formation in Mongolia's Gobi Desert and the Suba Shi Formation in the Xinjiang autonomous region of China.

ONE OF A KIND
The name *Tarbosaurus* was created to designate a new tyrannosaur nearly as large as *Tyrannosaurus* and very similar in detail. Some scientists believe these details are not important enough to deserve a new genus. They consider *Tarbosaurus bataar* to be a species within the genus *Tyrannosaurus*, i.e., *Tyrannosaurus bataar*. This may have some merit since strictly North American *Tyrannosaurus* and strictly Asian *Tarbosaurus* lived in places that were connected by a land bridge during the Late Cretaceous.

MORE FOSSIL EVIDENCE NEEDED
A 2003 study identified the tyrannosaur *Alioramus* as *Tarbosaurus'* closest known relative. If correct, this relationship would cast doubt on the *Tarbosaurus/Tyrannosaurus* link, lending support to the idea that separate tyrannosaur family lines evolved in North America and Asia. But some scientists think that the single known specimen of *Alioramus* is clearly separate from *Tarbosaurus*. More fossils are needed to resolve this issue.

TIMELINE (millions of years ago)

| 0 | 505 | 438 | 408 | 360 | 280 | 248 | 208 | 146 | 65 | 1.8 to today |

Tarbosaurus

• **ORDER** • Saurischia • **FAMILY** • Tyrannosauridae • **GENUS & SPECIES** • *Tarbosaurus bataar*

NEW FIND IN THE GOBI DESERT

Paleontology is an ongoing process and new things are discovered all the time. In 2006, a joint project between members of the Center of Paleontology at the Mongolian Academy of Sciences and experts from the Hayashibara Company, a biotechnology firm from Okayama, Japan, made an exciting find. The team discovered a nearly intact skeleton of a *Tarbosaurus* contained in a block of sandstone. The skeleton belonged to a young *Tarbosaurus* and is one of the best-preserved fossils of its kind ever discovered. The only parts missing were the neck bones and bones at the tip of the dinosaur's tail. The find was very important because the skeletons of young dinosaurs are often found in poor condition, eroded by weather or destroyed by predators. The *Tarbosaurus*, the gender of which is not known yet, measures 6.5 ft (2 m) long, one-sixth the estimated size of an adult. It was approximately five years old when it died around 70 million years ago.

Majungasaurus

• **ORDER** • Saurischia • **FAMILY** • Abelisauridae • **GENUS & SPECIES** • *Majungasaurus crenatissi*

VITAL STATISTICS

FOSSIL LOCATION	Madagascar
DIET	Carnivorous
PRONUNCIATION	Mah-JOONG-ah-THOL-us
WEIGHT	Unknown
LENGTH	26–30 ft (8–9 m)
HEIGHT	Unknown
MEANING OF NAME	"Majunga lizard" after the Majunga district of northern Madagascar, where the fossil was discovered

FOSSIL EVIDENCE

When it was first discovered, *Majungasaurus* material was mislabeled as a boneheaded dinosaur and named *Majungatholus*. The mistake was corrected in 1998 with the discovery of one of the most complete dinosaur skulls ever found. Now known to be a theropod, *Majungasaurus* is also one of the few dinosaurs where there is evidence of cannibalism, when an animal eats another animal of its kind. It may simply have scavenged dead bodies, rather than actively pursuing its own kind, or it may have cannibalized defeated rivals, but numerous bones have been found with tooth marks.

DINOSAUR

LATE CRETACEOUS

Majungasaurus was a predator that probably caught its victims in its broad snout, holding on until they were subdued — like modern cats. It was the top predator in its environment.

SKULL
Majungasaurus had a rough, textured skull, thick bone on top of its snout, and a single rounded horn above its eyes.

WHERE IN THE WORLD?

Majungasaurus was located in Madagascar, which was then joined to South America and India by a landbridge.

HOW BIG IS IT?

LEGS
Its front limbs are not complete in the fossil record but are very short, while its hind legs were longer and stocky.

TIMELINE (millions of years ago)

540	505	438	408	360	280	248	208	146	65	1.8 to today

Glossary

anatomy (uh-NA-duh-mee) The bodily structure of an animal or plant

bipedal (by-PED-ul) An animal that walks on two feet

cannibalism (KAN-ih-bul-izm) When one animal eats another animal of the same kind, such as a human eating another human

conical (KON-ih-kul) Shaped like a cone

endocast (EN-doh-kast) A model of the inside of a skull which shows the shape of the brain

estuaries (ES-chuw-air-ez) Water passage where a larger sea meets a river

femur (FEE-mur) A bone between the hip and the knee

fenestrae (feh-NES-tree) Hollow openings in the bone

fossil (FAH-sil) Remains or traces of an organism from the past that have been preserved, such as bones, teeth, footprints, etc.

piscivorous (pih-si-ver-us) A creature that eats fish

profusely (pro-FYUS-lee) A lot; gushing without any restraint

scimitar (SI-mih-tur) Sword with a slightly curving blade

serrated (seh-RAY-ted) Notched or toothed on the edge

sickle (SIH-kul) A tool with a half-moon shaped curved blade and a short handle

theropod (THIR-a-pod) A type of dinosaur with two feet and two smaller arms

trackway (TRAK-way) A series of fossil footprints

Index

For More Information

Books

Keiran, Monique. *Albertosaurus: Death of a Predator.* Vancouver, BC: Raincoast Books, 2002.

Malam, John. *Dinosaur.* New York: DK Publishing, 2006.

Manning, Phillip. *Dinomummy.* London, Kingfisher, 2007.

Web Sites

To ensure the currency and safety of recommended Internet links, Windmill maintains and updates an online list of sites related to the subject of this book. To access this list of Web sites, please go to www.windmillbooks.com/weblinks and select this book's title.

For more great fiction and nonfiction, go to www.windmillbooks.com.